THE
TOMATO
COOKBOOK

THE
TOMATO
COOKBOOK

VICTORIA LLOYD-DAVIES

SMITHMARK

This edition published in 1994 by
SMITHMARK Publishers Inc.,
16 East 32nd Street,
New York, NY 10016.

Copyright © Salamander Books Limited, 1994

1 3 5 7 9 8 6 4 2

SMITHMARK books are available for bulk purchase for sales promotion
and premium use. For details write or call the manager of special sales,
SMITHMARK Publishers Inc.,
16 East 32nd Street,
New York, NY 10016;
(212) 532-6600.

ISBN 0-8317-8661-2

CREDITS

COMMISSIONING EDITOR: *Will Steeds*
EDITOR: *Miranda Spicer*
DESIGN: *The Design Revolution, Brighton*
PHOTOGRAPHER: *Simon Butcher*
HOME ECONOMIST: *Wendy Dines*
STYLIST: *Marion Price*
COLOR SEPARATION: *P & W Graphics Pte Ltd*

Printed in Singapore

Library of Congress Cataloging-in-Publication Data

Lloyd-Davies, Victoria.
    The tomato cookbook / Victoria Lloyd-Davies.
        p. cm.
    Includes index.
    ISBN 0-8317-8661-2
    1. Cookery (Tomatoes) I. Title.
    TX803.T6L56 1994   94-30358
    641.6'5642--dc20   CIP

ABOUT THE INGREDIENTS

As seasoning is a matter of personal taste, salt and pepper are not
necessarily listed in the ingredients.
Try to obtain the best quality fresh produce.

CONTENTS

The fragrant smell of fresh garden tomatoes always reminds me of summer. Nothing can beat a sliced tomato salad sprinkled with a little chopped basil, a pinch of both sugar and ground black pepper and a drizzle of extra-virgin olive oil. A glass of chilled white wine and some freshly baked crusty bread turns this simple dish into a summer meal. Second on my list of favorites is a freshly made tomato sandwich served with a cup of tea. Although the simplest dishes are often the best, so many can be cooked with this versatile vegetable.

My early adult summers were spent on the Adriatic coast of southern Italy. As I was the only "trained cook" at my uncle's house, it was left to me to do most of the cooking. I remember the tomato–laden trucks winding their way over the mountains to Naples, and the boxes of warm plum tomatoes in the local village stores. I used them constantly; raw in salads at lunchtime and cooked in sauces with pasta, fish, poultry and meat in the evenings. I never weighed them. With the help of this constant supply of tomatoes, I was able to turn very simple ideas into beautiful, rich red, tasty dishes. The secret is not to be stingy with tomatoes in cooking; use a plentiful supply.

More recently I have spent vacations in the Greek islands. I return with fond memories of going into taverna kitchens to choose our family meals and seeing roasting pans filled with enormous stuffed tomatoes. They are wonderful when freshly cooked and hot.

I have brought together a fund of tomato recipes for *The Tomato Cookbook*. Many are family favorites with ideas for special occasions. Fresh tomatoes dominate but some of my recipes feature sun-dried tomatoes to strengthen the flavor; others use convenient products such as canned tomatoes, purées you can buy in cartons and pastes. I have tried to include a large variety of recipes, ranging from attractive and enticing hot or cold appetizers to robust chutneys and pickles.

Today, we see many varieties of tomatoes coming into our stores. The traditional round tomato is still popular, but now there are many different sizes and flavors to choose from. The new cherry tomatoes are so sweet you can pop them into your mouth like candy. Put a bowlful out with drinks alongside the traditional nibbles. Buy plenty of them as you will be refilling the bowl more than once! Look out for the yellow cherry tomatoes as well as the red.

Although I had seen tomatoes growing in garden greenhouses and in the fields of Italy and Greece, I had never seen tomato growing in my native Britain on a large scale until I started to write this book. When I walked into the magnificent hothouses, I came across the lovely smell of the tomato plants and the gentle hum of the bees as they went about their work pollinating the tomato flowers. I have also discovered a few tips about handling tomatoes, their preparation and their cooking. I have passed these on to you in a hints and tips section on page 12, and I hope these will be useful and will help you to enjoy the recipes. One of the main points to remember is that tomatoes are a subtropical fruit. They hate the cold, especially the refrigerator. To enjoy them at their best, serve them at room temperature. I keep tomatoes in the fruit bowl!

Victoria Lloyd-David

Introduction

The tomato is a berry and therefore a fruit but we use it as a vegetable. Tomatoes originate from South America. They were first cultivated by the Aztecs in the 16th century. Stories abound on how the tomato traveled from South America to southern Europe. Some say a Spanish priest brought seeds to Seville from Peru. Another legend tells us two Jesuit priests brought them to Italy from Mexico, and that the first tomatoes were yellow, earning them the Italian name *pomi d'oro* – golden apples. Southern Italy is still a big growing area and Italian cooking is based on *pomodora* – tomato dishes. The origin of the English word tomato comes from the Spanish word *tomate*. The French, convinced that the red berries had aphrodisiac qualities, called them *pomme d'amour* – love apples. Today, they are the most widely available vegetable in the world, grown all over the world, from as far north as Iceland to the Southern tip of New Zealand. Tomatoes were first grown for their decorative leaves rather than their fruit. For many years tomatoes were grown in Britain and throughout Europe as ornamental climbers. The first tomato grower on record in the UK was Patrick Bellow of Castletown who successfully reared plants from seeds in 1554. The Elizabethans thought the bright red color of the fruit was a danger signal and that tomatoes were therefore harmful.

Cultivated Tomatoes

It was not until the 19th century that commercial cultivation began. The first hothouses were built in Kent and Essex, in England, in the mid-19th century when large scale production of sheet glass became possible. Today, commercial hothouses cover vast areas of agricultural land. The largest single hothouse, which covers 22 acres, is in the *Guinness Book of Records*.

The hothouse offers a much longer growing season; it raises the temperature of the soil and air within; it provides shelter from the weather; and it protects the crop from birds and animals. The temperature, humidity, air, water, light and nutrients are all controlled to give ideal conditions. The plants are cultivated in the same way as in a garden greenhouse, except on a much larger scale. Walk into tomato hothouses in Britain and you will hear the gentle buzz of bumble bees pollinating the tomato flowers. Rows of tomato plants stretch into the distance. Each plant will be green and healthy with trusses of tomatoes hanging from its stem. The fruit requires 40 to 60 days from flowering to reach full ripeness. The first tomatoes ripen low down the plant

Above: A tomato plant.

ABOVE: The bumble bee is the natural pollinator most widely used by many tomato growers.

but as the season progresses, they ripen further up. All tomatoes are picked by hand. Predators are encouraged, rather than chemical sprays by some growers. Nature has created a bug-eat-bug world, so tomato growers have harnessed beneficial insects to control pests organically.

CHOOSING TOMATOES

Traditional round tomatoes are the most popular, accounting for over 80 percent of tomato sales. They are good for broiling, baking or frying as a vegetable, using as a cooking ingredient for soups and sauces or eating raw in salads.

Cherry tomatoes are much smaller than the traditional round tomatoes. Cherry tomatoes are the smallest, while hybrid **cocktail tomatoes** are slightly larger. Both are enjoyed for their sweetness and concentrated flavor. Cherry tomatoes are best eaten whole and raw in salads; cocktail tomatoes can be halved for salads or skewered whole for grilling. Most cherry tomatoes are red but yellow ones are also available.

Beefsteak, or beef, tomatoes are much larger than the traditional round tomato. Their size and shape makes them excellent for stuffing and baking whole.

Plum tomatoes have a distinctive oval shape with firm flesh and less liquid in the center. These are ideal for Mediterranean dishes such as pizza, pasta and salads. In fact, you will sometimes find them for sale labeled as Italian tomatoes.

Sun-dried tomatoes are dried naturally in the Californian or Mediterranean sun, then they are packed in glass jars with olive oil and sold as *pomodori secchi* or sun-dried tomatoes in oil. Others are packed dry in sealed cellophane bags. They can be added to hot or cold dishes, or simply spread over slices of Italian bread for a snack.

Canned, peeled tomatoes are probably one of the most popular convenience cooking ingredients. They are mainly plum tomatoes, often Italian and peeled, often crushed, and sometimes mixed with herbs, flavorings or vegetables, such as peppers, onions and garlic. One Italian tomato cannery has recently celebrated its centenary. There are plenty of other tomato products in gourmet stores and supermarkets.

Smooth, thick purées of strained tomatoes are sold in Italian delicatessens or gourmet food stores. They are natural in color and flavor and have no additives. Once opened, they should be stored in the refrigerator.

Tomato paste is a double concentrate form of tomatoes sold in small cans or tubes. Some specialists

ABOVE: (left to right) Cherry tomato, cocktail tomato, salad tomato, traditional round tomato, plum tomato, beefsteak tomato, Momatara beefsteak tomato.

ABOVE: (clockwise from top left) Strained purée, tomato juice, canned tomatoes, sun-dried tomatoes in oil, tomato flakes, sun-dried tomatoes, tomato purée.

make a paste with sun-dried tomatoes for an even more distinctive flavor. Tomato juice is sold in cartons or cans as a refreshing long drink, or in small cans or bottles for mixer drinks, aperitifs and cocktails.

Fresh tomato sauces can be found in supermarket chill cabinets.

BUYING TOMATOES

Tomatoes are available all year round. Choose firm tomatoes with bright, unflawed skins. They should be a good shape, good color and have a smooth skin. When cut, they should be firm to the center. There are two tests for freshness: one is the smell, which should be faintly aromatic; and the other is that the small gray-green leaves at the stem end (technically called the calyx) should not be too withered or dried. A ripe tomato will

yield slightly when gently pressed.

Just-ripe tomatoes are best stored at room temperature because they are a subtropical fruit and they prefer warmth. Never keep tomatoes in the refrigerator, even overripe ones, as they become soft quicker in cold temperatures. Buy tomatoes regularly, and if you have put them in a plastic bag, or if they are prepacked, remove this packaging and place them in a bowl. Handle tomatoes gently so you do not bruise the skins.

To ripen homegrown tomatoes, place a ripe tomato in with the unripe ones in a paper bag at room temperature. The ripe tomato will help ripen the others. Do not, however, put picked tomatoes in the sun to ripen because they will just become mushy. If you have a glut of overripe tomatoes, use them to make soups and sauces which can be stored in the freezer.

The end-of-the-season, yellow or green slightly underripe traditional round tomatoes are most suitable for making chutneys.

NUTRITION

Low in calories. Tomatoes contain about 93 calories per pound. Their low-calorie content is because they do not contain more than a trace of fat, although they are considered rich in sugar.

Good source of vitamins. Tomatoes are an excellent source of vitamin C, most of which is found in the soft, jelly-like substance around the seeds. Sun-ripened tomatoes can contain up to twice as much vitamin C as ones ripened in a hothouse. Heat often destroys vitamin C, which is a reason for eating tomatoes raw. Grilled tomatoes are high in carotene and folate.

Mineral content. Potassium and calcium together with mineral salts and trace elements. Grilled tomatoes contain a higher concentration of nutrients.

Dietary fiber. Tomato skin and seeds contribute dietary fiber to a diet when eaten raw.

Sodium content. Anyone on a low-sodium diet should avoid eating too many tinned tomatoes, unless the label specifically indicates they are low in sodium.

PREPARATION

For salads, remove the stem and rinse the tomatoes under cold running water. Dry them with paper towels. Before cooking whole tomatoes, make a cross in the skin over the top of the tomato with a sharp knife. This will prevent the skin from splitting.

To peel tomatoes, make a "nick" in the skin with a sharp knife. Then put in a bowl and, cover with boiling water for one minute, then drain and pour cold water over. Remove the tomatoes, one at a time, and remove the skins with a sharp knife. There is no need to remove the core unless the tomato is very big.

If a recipe requires the use of a tomato as a shell, take a slice off the top of the tomato or slice it in half, then gently scoop out the seeds with a teaspoon. Season the inside of the tomato. Turn it upside down onto a piece of paper towel to let the juices drain off. Dry inside the tomato shell with a paper towel.

Some recipes specify using a tomato purée which has had the seeds removed so it is really smooth. To do this, use a fine nylon or stainless-steel strainer and press the tomato pulp through the mesh with a wooden spoon. Or you can buy cartons of puréed and strained tomatoes that are ready to use at Italian food stores.

Homemade tomato juice is quick and easy to make. Chop the tomatoes, then purée them in a blender or food processor. Strain the juice through a fine strainer.

Peeled and seeded tomatoes make excellent pulp or purée for cooking, so it is a good idea to take advantage of a glut and stock the freezer. Cook them slowly until reduced to the required consistency. Leave them to cool, then pour into freezer bags or ice-cube trays and freeze. Once frozen, transfer the cubes to freezer bags. These can be stored in the freezer for up to six months and used for soups, sauces and casseroles.

Tomatoes also make attractive garnishes. Always use a sharp paring knife. To make a **tomato flower**, make a series of "v" shaped cuts or zigzags around the middle of each tomato, pushing the knife tip right through to the center. Carefully pull the two halves apart.

To make a **tomato rose**, cut a slice from the bottom of the tomato and continue peeling off the skin in a spiral, taking care not to break the skin. Place the strip on a flat surface and loosely wind it to form a neat roll like the bottom of a rose and secure with a toothpick. Wind a second piece of skin tightly to form the center of the rose. Place it in the middle and secure with a toothpick.

ABOVE: *(top) Tomato tulip; (left) tomato flower; (right) tomato rose.*

For a **tomato tulip**, make six diagonal cuts into the skin from the core to half way down the tomato. Peel back the skin with a sharp knife.

The only preparation needed before using sun-dried tomatoes in oil is to drain them before use. The remaining oil can be used in the recipe or in a stir fry or saved for a salad dressing mixed with a little balsamic vinegar. However, dried sun-dried tomatoes require soaking before use. Follow the package directions, but if you buy them loose from a delicatessen the general rule is to rinse them well, then soak them in warm water for 20 minutes. Strain, then use them on their own or with fresh tomatoes. Once opened, it is best to transfer the remaining dried tomatoes to a screw-top jar and store them in the refrigerator. If the tomatoes are very tough or salty, refresh them in a few changes of hot water.

HINTS AND TIPS

☉ Always keep tomatoes at room temperature and not in the refrigerator. They are a subtropical fruit and they dislike the cold. Prepare salad tomatoes at least four hours before the meal.

☉ The natural herb partners for tomatoes are mint, parsley, basil and oregano. For the best flavor, use fresh herbs rather than dried.

☉ Season tomatoes with a pinch of sugar to bring out their natural sweetness.

☉ If a recipe requires the removal of seeds and juices, reserve these and use for making stocks and sauces.

☉ Always drain tomato shells on paper towels and dry them out well before filling them.

☉ Tomatoes give food a good color. Add some tomato paste to pale chicken or fish dishes.

☉ Always use a sharp knife to cut tomatoes. One with a fine serrated edge can be used as an alternative.

☉ If tomatoes are cooked with their skins on they retain more flavor.

☉ Put whole or halved tomatoes on skewers for a barbecue. Team them with other vegetables which cook quickly, such as mushrooms, peppers and zucchini.

☉ Tomato seeds give a good texture to soups and sauces but if the recipe requires a smooth purée, it is important to strain the purée. Because tomatoes are an acid fruit, use a nylon or stainless steel strainer.

☉ Make a cross in the skin of the tomato before baking. Press a little crushed garlic or chopped herbs into the tomato, drizzle some olive oil over and cook at 375°F 15 to 20 minutes.

☉ Brush the tomatoes with oil or sprinkle some bread crumbs over before broiling. Broil tomatoes slowly, otherwise the cut surface will begin to burn before the tomato is heated through.

☉ Tomatoes get particularly hot in the microwave and in toasted sandwiches. Leave to cool slightly before eating.

☉ Use sun-dried tomatoes in conjunction with fresh tomatoes to strengthen the tomato flavor of the dish.

☉ Put some halved tomatoes around roasted meat for the last 20 minutes of cooking time.

☉ Serve tomato juice with lots of ice. Add a dash of lemon juice, Worcestershire or hot-pepper sauce.

☉ Tomato juice is an excellent pick-me-up after a heavy night's eating and drinking.

☉ To turn tomato soup into a meal, cover it with a thick layer of grated mozzarella cheese and lots of chopped fresh basil. Serve with large slices of crusty bread.

☉ Homemade tomato soups and sauces can be stored in the freezer for up to six months.

☉ Use under-ripe or green tomatoes for making chutneys and pickles.

RIGHT: Tomato soup covered with a thick layer of mozzarella cheese and chopped fresh basil, served with crusty bread.

Soups and Appetizers

"Real" tomato soup made with fresh tomatoes is easy to make and tastes delicious. Because tomatoes work equally well hot or cold, they make tasty soups, mousses, dips and pâtés, or can be stuffed with meat or vegetable fillings.

Classic Tomato Soup

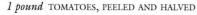

2 tablespoons OLIVE OIL
2 pounds TOMATOES, HALVED
2 cloves GARLIC
SALT AND PEPPER
1 SMALL POTATO, PEELED AND SLICED
1 teaspoon SUGAR

To garnish
4 teaspoons LIGHT CREAM
sprig PARSLEY

Preheat the oven to 375°F. Lightly oil a roasting pan. Arrange the tomatoes, cut sides up in the roasting pan. Add the garlic cloves. Season and drizzle the remaining oil over. Roast for 30 minutes.

Meanwhile, boil the potato in 1¼ cups water until tender; reserve the potato water. Skin the tomatoes and garlic. Purée the tomato pulp and garlic in a blender or food processor with the potato and potato stock until smooth. Transfer to a pan. Add a little extra stock or water if too thick. Stir in the sugar and cream. Garnish and serve. SERVES 4

Tomato and Orange Soup with Basil

1 pound TOMATOES, PEELED AND HALVED
1 ONION, SLICED
1 CARROT, SLICED
1 strip LEMON PEEL
1 BAY LEAF
2 teaspoons CHOPPED FRESH BASIL OR
½ teaspoon DRIED BASIL
2 ½ cups VEGETABLE STOCK
2 tablespoons BUTTER
¼ cup ALL-PURPOSE FLOUR
1 SMALL ORANGE

Squeeze the tomatoes to remove the seeds. Put the tomatoes, onion and carrot in a pan with the lemon peel, bay leaf and basil. Season. Add stock and simmer, covered, for 30 minutes. Purée and set aside.

Clean the pan, melt the butter, add the flour and cook for a few minutes. Remove from the heat, then gradually add the puréed mixture. Bring to a boil to thicken. Peel the orange. Shred the peel finely and blanch, then refresh in cold water. Squeeze the orange and add the juice to the soup. Check the seasoning and serve garnished with orange peel. SERVES 4

RIGHT: Classic Tomato Soup

CHILLED TOMATO SOUP

1 pound TOMATOES, PEELED AND THINLY SLICED
4 SCALLIONS, THINLY SLICED
4 cloves GARLIC, FINELY CHOPPED
1 strip LEMON PEEL
3 tablespoons TOMATO PASTE
2 tablespoons ALL-PURPOSE FLOUR
2 1/2 cups CHICKEN STOCK
1 teaspoon HOT-PEPPER SAUCE
1 teaspoon SUGAR
2 tablespoons SHERRY (OPTIONAL)
1 teaspoon LEMON JUICE
2/3 cup LIGHT CREAM
thin slices CUCUMBER, TO GARNISH

Put the tomatoes, scallions, garlic, lemon peel and 4 tablespoons water in a saucepan. Simmer gently for 10 - 15 minutes. Add the tomato paste and cook for 3 minutes longer. Make a paste with the flour and some of the stock, then stir it in. Add the remaining stock, hot-pepper sauce and sugar. Season. Bring to a boil, stirring. Strain the soup through a fine strainer. Add sherry (if desired) and the lemon juice. Add the cream and refrigerate until very cold. Serve chilled garnished with thin cucumber slices. SERVES 6-8

GAZPACHO

1 CUCUMBER
1 pound TOMATOES, PEELED
1 large GREEN BELL PEPPER, SEEDED
1 ONION
1 clove GARLIC, CRUSHED
3-4 tablespoons OIL
3-4 tablespoons WINE VINEGAR
1 3/4 cups TOMATO JUICE
2 tablespoons TOMATO PASTE

Roughly chop the cucumber, tomatoes, pepper and onion. Reserve some vegetables for the garnish and chop these more finely. Put the roughly chopped vegetables and garlic into a bowl. Add the remaining ingredients. Purée in small amounts in a blender or food processor. Pour into a bowl. Cover and chill well. Serve in soup bowls garnished with the reserved vegetables.

SERVES 6

TOP: *Chilled Tomato Soup*
BOTTOM: *Gazpacho*

QUICK STUFFED TOMATOES

6 LARGE TOMATOES
2 RIPE AVOCADOS
1/2 cup CREAM CHEESE
1 teaspoon HORSERADISH SAUCE
1 teaspoon LEMON JUICE
1 teaspoon GARLIC PASTE
SALT AND PEPPER
6 slices RYE BREAD

Use a sharp knife to remove the top of each tomato. Scoop out the flesh with a small teaspoon. Halve the avocados, remove the seeds and scoop out the flesh.

Place the avocados in a small bowl with the cream cheese and horseradish sauce. Beat until smooth. Add lemon juice and garlic paste and seasoning.

Place in a decorating bag with a small star piping tip. Fill the tomatoes with the avocado mixture and place each one on a base of rye bread. Pipe the remaining avocado mixture around the bottom of each tomato. Serve at room temperature. SERVES 6

HOT STUFFED TOMATOES

4 BEEFSTEAK TOMATOES
1 tablespoon OLIVE OIL
1 ONION, PEELED AND FINELY CHOPPED
1 small clove GARLIC, CRUSHED
2 stalks CELERY, FINELY CHOPPED
3/4 cup FRESH WHOLE-WHEAT BREAD CRUMBS
1 tablespoon CHOPPED FRESH HERBS (BASIL, OREGANO, MARJORAM)
SALT AND PEPPER

Preheat the oven to 350°F. Stand the tomatoes on their stem ends and slice off the top quarter. Remove the pulp with a small spoon and reserve. Stand the tomatoes upside down on paper towels to drain.

Heat the oil in a pan and fry the onion, garlic and celery until soft but not browned. Stir in the bread crumbs, herbs and tomato pulp. Season well. Fill the tomato cases with the mixture and replace the tops. Bake for about 20 minutes. Serve hot. SERVES 4

RIGHT: Hot Stuffed Tomatoes

CHERRY TOMATOES WITH RED BELL PEPPER AND ORANGE

Look in delicatessens or gourmet food stores for packages of aspic powder, also sometimes called aspic jelly.

1 RED BELL PEPPER, SEEDED AND QUARTERED
3/4-ounce ENVELOPE ASPIC POWDER
1 LARGE ORANGE, GRATED PEEL RESERVED
2 teaspoons CORIANDER SEEDS, TOASTED
9 ounces CHERRY TOMATOES, RESERVE 3, PEEL AND SLICE REMAINDER
few sprigs FRESH CHERVIL
1 cup TOMATO JUICE
ORANGE SLICES AND FRESH CHERVIL, TO GARNISH

Broil the pepper until charred. Place in a plastic bag and set aside for 20 minutes, then peel and cut into strips.

Dissolve the aspic powder in 1 cup boiling water. Stir the grated orange peel into the aspic. Place a spoonful of aspic in the bottom of 6 individual molds or ramekins. Chill until set. Crush the coriander seeds.

Slice the reserved tomatoes into wedges and arrange on the aspic with the chervil. Carefully spoon a little more aspic over. Chill until set. Make the aspic up to 1 3/4 cups with the tomato juice and stir in the coriander seeds. Arrange the orange pieces on top of the aspic and spoon a little tomato aspic over. Chill until set. Layer the tomatoes on top of the oranges with the red pepper and tomato aspic. Chill until set.

To serve, dip the molds in hot water for a few seconds, invert onto plates and garnish. SERVES 6

TOMATO AND LIME MOUSSE

Italian food stores and some delicatessens sell cartons of puréed and strained tomatoes, which will save you time.

2 large EGGS, SEPARATED
3/4 cup plus 2 tablespoons PURÉED AND STRAINED TOMATOES
3 tablespoons TOMATO PASTE
grated peel and juice of 1 LARGE LIME
1 tablespoon UNFLAVORED GELATIN
1 cup plus 2 tablespoons MASCARPONE CHEESE
2 tablespoons CHOPPED FRESH CILANTRO
SALT AND PEPPER
LIME SLICES AND FRESH CILANTRO, TO GARNISH

Sauce
1 pound TOMATOES, PEELED, SEEDED AND CHOPPED
1 clove GARLIC, CRUSHED
2 tablespoons OLIVE OIL
1 sprig PARSLEY

Beat the egg yolks into the strained tomatoes. Cook over low heat until the mixture thickens. Do not boil. Beat in the tomato paste and lime peel. Sprinkle the gelatin onto the lime juice. Leave to soak for 5 minutes, then dissolve over a pan of hot water. Cool. Beat gelatin mixture into tomato mixture with cheese and cilantro. Season. When beginning to set, beat egg whites until stiff, then fold into tomato mixture. Turn into a wetted 9- x 5- x 3-inch bread pan; chill until set.

Put all the sauce ingredients in a saucepan. Season. Cover and simmer for 30 minutes. Remove the parsley, then strain the mixture sinto a jug. Chill.

Dip the loaf pan into hot water for a few seconds, then invert onto a board. Slice the mousse, garnish and serve with the chilled tomato sauce. SERVES 6

TOP: Cherry Tomatoes with Red Pepper and Orange

BOTTOM: Tomato and Lime Mousse

GUACAMOLE

2 RIPE AVOCADOS, SEEDED AND PEELED
2 *tablespoons* LEMON JUICE
2 *tablespoons* VERY FINELY CHOPPED SCALLION
2 *cloves* GARLIC, CRUSHED
1/4-1/2 *teaspoon* HOT-PEPPER SAUCE
pinch CHILI POWDER
2 TOMATOES, PEELED, SEEDED AND
VERY FINELY CHOPPED

TORTILLA CHIPS, TO SERVE

Mash the avocados into a purée with the lemon juice. Stir in the remaining ingredients. Turn into a serving dish, cover with plastic wrap and refrigerate for 1 hour. Serve with tortilla chips.   SERVES 4-6

SUN-DRIED TOMATO AND GOAT CHEESE PÂTÉ

3 *ounces* SUN-DRIED TOMATOES IN OIL,
DRAINED
8 *ounces* SOFT GOAT CHEESE
1/3 *cup* PECAN NUTS OR WALNUTS, ROUGHLY
CHOPPED
To serve
FRESHLY CHOPPED BASIL
CIABATTA BREAD, TOASTED OR
WHOLE-GRAIN BREAD

Place two-thirds of the tomatoes and the goat cheese in a blender or food processor and blend until almost smooth. Add the remaining tomatoes and blend to break them up, but allow them to remain textured. Transfer to a bowl and stir in the nuts. Stir to mix well. Turn the pâté into individual pâté dishes or into a serving dish. Chill.

To serve, sprinkle fresh basil on top of the pâté and accompany with toasted ciabatta or whole-grain bread.

SERVES 4

TOP: Guacamole

BOTTOM: Sun-dried Tomato and Goat Cheese Pâté

SALADS

Always serve tomatoes for eating raw at room temperature. Bring out their natural sweetness with a pinch of sugar and choose a dressing which will not smother their flavor. Drizzle a good-quality olive oil over and add freshly chopped herbs.

CLASSIC TOMATO SALAD

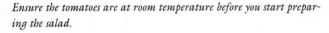

Ensure the tomatoes are at room temperature before you start preparing the salad.

1 pound	TOMATOES
1/2 teaspoon	SUGAR
1/4 teaspoon	SALT
1/4 teaspoon	GROUND BLACK PEPPER
2 tablespoons	EXTRA-VIRGIN OLIVE OIL
2 teaspoons	WHITE-WINE VINEGAR
1 tablespoon	SNIPPED FRESH CHIVES

Thinly slice the tomatoes, discarding ends, and arrange on a plate. Sprinkle the sugar, salt and pepper over. Set aside for 30 minutes at room temperature. Beat the oil and vinegar together and drizzle over the tomatoes. Sprinkle the chives over. Leave for another 30 minutes before serving.   SERVES 4

TOMATO AND MOZZARELLA SALAD

2 tablespoons	PINE NUTS (OPTIONAL)
1 1/2 pounds	TOMATOES
12 ounces	MOZZARELLA CHEESE
2 tablespoons	BASIL LEAVES
4 tablespoons	EXTRA-VIRGIN OLIVE OIL

Toast the pine nuts (if using) until pale golden in a dry skillet over medium heat, stirring constantly. Slice the tomatoes and mozzarella cheese. Arrange on serving plates and season. Chop the larger basil leaves, or keep small leaves whole, then scatter them over the tomatoes and cheese. Drizzle the olive oil over. Sprinkle on the toasted pine nuts if desired. Serve with warm Italian ciabatta bread or French bread.   SERVES 4

TOP: Classic Tomato Salad
BOTTOM: Tomato and Mozzarella Salad

MEDITERRANEAN TRICOLOR SALAD

2 GREEN BELL PEPPERS
2 RED BELL PEPPERS
2 YELLOW BELL PEPPERS

Dressing
6 *tablespoons* OLIVE OIL
2 *tablespoons* RED-WINE VINEGAR
2 *cloves* GARLIC, CRUSHED
SALT AND PEPPER

To serve
1 *pound* BEEFSTEAK TOMATOES
4 BASIL LEAVES, SHREDDED

Broil the peppers until the skin is blistered and charred, turning them so they blister all around. Place them in a plastic bag and set aside for 20 minutes. Peel off the skins, cut away the cores and discard the seeds. Slice the peppers and put them in a dish. Beat all the dressing ingredients together. Season. Pour over the peppers and leave to marinate for 1 hour.

Slice the tomatoes and arrange on a serving dish. Pile the peppers in the center and scatter the shredded basil leaves over.

SERVES 4

MEXICAN SALAD WITH CHILI DRESSING

2 LARGE ORANGES
4 SMALL HEADS BELGIAN ENDIVE
4 LARGE TOMATOES
1 SMALL GREEN CHILI, SEEDED

sprigs FRESH DILL, TO GARNISH

Dressing
3 *tablespoons* PLAIN YOGURT
3 *tablespoons* MAYONNAISE
1-2 *teaspoons* CHILI SAUCE
pinch CHILI POWDER

Peel the oranges and remove the white pith. Cut the oranges into thin slices, discarding any seeds. Cut the heads of endive in half lengthwise. Cut the tomatoes into wedges. Arrange the orange slices, endive spears and tomatoes on 4 individual plates. Chop the chili and sprinkle over the top. Mix all the dressing ingredients together and spoon a little over each salad. Serve any remaining dressing separately. Garnish with dill.

SERVES 4

RIGHT: Mediterranean Tricolor Salad

TOMATO AND ENDIVE SALAD

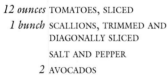

1 pound CHERRY TOMATOES, QUARTERED
1 head BELGIAN ENDIVE

Dressing
3 tablespoons WALNUT OIL
1 tablespoon BALSAMIC VINEGAR
juice of 1/2 LEMON
1/2 teaspoon SUGAR
SALT AND PEPPER

Put the tomatoes in a bowl. Slice the Belgian endive, discarding the end. Add the sliced endive to the tomatoes. Beat the dressing ingredients together and pour over the tomatoes. Season. Leave to marinate for 1 hour. SERVES 4

WARM TOMATO SALAD

2 tablespoons OLIVE OIL
1 pound CHERRY TOMATOES
1 teaspoon SUGAR
MIXED GREEN SALAD FOR 4 SERVINGS
1 tablespoon BALSAMIC VINEGAR

Heat the oil in a skillet. Add the tomatoes and sugar and stir and shake over medium heat for 2-3 minutes until the tomato skins begin to split. Spoon the tomatoes over the green salad. Sprinkle the vinegar over. Toss and serve immediately. SERVES 4

TOMATO AND AVOCADO SALAD

12 ounces TOMATOES, SLICED
1 bunch SCALLIONS, TRIMMED AND DIAGONALLY SLICED
SALT AND PEPPER
2 AVOCADOS
juice of 1 LEMON

Dressing
3 tablespoons OLIVE OIL
2 tablespoons RED-WINE VINEGAR
2 teaspoons HONEY
2 teaspoons DIJON MUSTARD

Put the tomatoes and scallions in a bowl and season. Peel the avocados, halve, remove the seeds and slice. Squeeze the lemon juice over to prevent them from browning. Gently mix the avocados with the tomatoes and onions. Put the olive oil, red-wine vinegar, honey and mustard in a screw-top jar, then shake vigorously to mix. Gently toss into the salad and serve. SERVES 4

TOP: *Tomato and Endive Salad*
BOTTOM: *Warm Tomato Salad*

PASTA SALAD

☙

1 cup PASTA SHAPES
SALT AND PEPPER
6 ounces CHERRY TOMATOES, HALVED
8 ounces TOMATOES, PEELED
2 SMALL ZUCCHINI, THINLY SLICED
1 tablespoon SHREDDED BASIL LEAVES

Dressing
4 tablespoons OLIVE OIL
1 tablespoon RED-WINE VINEGAR
1 clove GARLIC, CRUSHED

Cook the pasta in boiling salted water for about 5 minutes until *al dente*. Drain and rinse in cold water, then drain again. Put the pasta in a bowl with the cherry tomatoes. Quarter the other tomatoes and remove seeds, then cut each quarter in half. Add to the salad with the zucchini. Mix the dressing and season to taste, then pour over the salad. Cover and chill for 1 hour in the refrigerator. Just before serving, stir in the shredded basil. SERVES 6

CHERRY TOMATO AND BLUE CHEESE SALAD

☙

8 ounces BACON SLICES
1 ROUND HEAD LETTUCE
1 pound CHERRY TOMATOES
1 bunch WATERCRESS
2 AVOCADOS
juice of 1 LEMON
8 ounces GORGONZOLA CHEESE, FINELY SLICED
4 tablespoons OLIVE OIL
2 tablespoons RED-WINE VINEGAR
2 teaspoons HONEY
1 teaspoon MUSTARD
SALT AND PEPPER

Fry the bacon until crisp and drain on paper towels, then finely chop. Separate, wash and dry the lettuce. Halve the tomatoes. Trim and wash the watercress. Mix the bacon, lettuce, tomatoes and watercress together. Peel and slice the avocados, then squeeze the lemon juice over to stop them browning. Toss into the salad. Gently stir the cheese into the salad. Mix the olive oil and red-wine vinegar. Add the honey and mustard and season. Toss into the salad. Arrange on serving plates and scatter the crispy bacon pieces over. SERVES 4

RIGHT: Cherry Tomato and Blue Cheese Salad

SANDWICHES AND SNACKS

The tomato is a truly portable food and is ideal for taking on picnics. Sandwiches can be made using tomato breads, which include tomatoes baked in the dough. The chapter also includes bagels, muffins and toasted sandwiches – plenty of ideas for snacks, brunches and lunch boxes.

BLT

1 slice BACON
1 tablespoon LOW-FAT SPREAD
2 slices WHOLE-GRAIN BREAD
2 teaspoons MAYONNAISE
1 TOMATO, SLICED
2 BOSTON LETTUCE LEAVES

Fry the bacon until it is really crisp. Cool on paper towels, then cut in half. Spread low-fat spread on one side of each slice of bread. Repeat with the mayonnaise. Arrange the bacon on one slice of bread, top with the sliced tomato and lettuce leaves. Put the other slice of bread on top. Press down gently and cut sandwich into 2 triangles.

MAKES 1 SANDWICH

SMOKED SALMON AND TOMATO BAGEL

1 BAGEL
1 tablespoon MASCARPONE CHEESE
1 ounce SMOKED SALMON
1 TOMATO, THINLY SLICED
GROUND BLACK PEPPER
2 sprigs FRESH DILL

Slice the bagel in half horizontally. Spread both sides with mascarpone cheese. Top 1 side with smoked salmon, tomato, black pepper and dill. Place the other half of the bagel on top.

SERVES 1

TOP: BLT

BOTTOM: Smoked Salmon and Tomato Bagel

TOASTED GRUYÈRE AND TOMATO SANDWICH

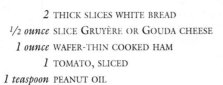

2 THICK SLICES WHITE BREAD
1/2 ounce SLICE GRUYÈRE OR GOUDA CHEESE
1 ounce WAFER-THIN COOKED HAM
1 TOMATO, SLICED
1 teaspoon PEANUT OIL

Preheat a sandwich toaster. Meanwhile, place a slice of bread down on a board, top with the cheese and then the ham, followed by sliced tomato. Place the second slice of bread on top and press down firmly. Lightly oil the heated sandwich toaster. Place sandwich in toaster. Cover and toast for approximately 3 minutes or until the bread is golden and crisp.   MAKES 1 SANDWICH

TOMATO AND MUSHROOM ENGLISH MUFFINS

1 1/2 cups SLICED CLOSED-CUP MUSHROOMS
1 teaspoon WORCESTERSHIRE SAUCE
1 teaspoon WHOLE-GRAIN MUSTARD
1 WHOLE-WHEAT MUFFIN
2 TOMATOES, SLICED

Put the mushrooms, 2 tablespoons water, the Worcestershire sauce and mustard together in a small saucepan. Simmer over low heat, stirring occasionally.

Meanwhile, preheat the broiler. Split the muffin in half and toast under the broiler on both sides. Top each half with sliced tomato and broil until heated through. Spoon the mushroom mixture over the tops.   MAKES 2

RIGHT: Tomato and Mushroom English Muffins

EGGPLANT AND MOZZARELLA BITES

It is important that the eggplant and tomatoes are approximately the same circumference when sliced.

1 EGGPLANT
SALT AND PEPPER
4 tablespoons PURÉED AND STRAINED TOMATOES
1 cup GRATED MOZZARELLA CHEESE
2 BEEFSTEAK TOMATOES, PEELED AND SLICED
10-12 BASIL LEAVES
1 tablespoon OLIVE OIL

Slice the eggplant into $1/2$-inch slices. Sprinkle with salt and set aside for 30 minutes. Rinse, drain and dry with paper towels.

Preheat the oven to 425°F. Arrange the eggplant slices on a greased baking sheet. Spread 1 teaspoon of the strained tomatoes on each eggplant slice. Top with mozzarella, tomato slices and basil leaves. Season. Drizzle a little oil over each basil leaf. Bake for 15 minutes. Cool for 1 minute before serving.

MAKES 10-12

CROSTINI

$1^1/2$ pounds PLUM TOMATOES, PEELED, SEEDED AND FINELY CHOPPED
3 cloves GARLIC, FINELY CHOPPED
8 BASIL LEAVES, CHOPPED
4 tablespoons EXTRA-VIRGIN OLIVE OIL
3 ANCHOVIES, DRAINED AND FINELY CHOPPED
1 cup PITTED AND FINELY CHOPPED RIPE OLIVES
1 loaf CIABATTA BREAD
1 cup GRATED MOZZARELLA CHEESE

Put the tomatoes, garlic and basil in a bowl. Add the olive oil and stir well. Marinate at room temperature for 1 hour.

Preheat the oven to 400°F. Stir the anchovies and olives into the bowl with the tomato mixture. Cut the bread into thick slices. Arrange the slices on a baking sheet. Bake for 10 minutes. Remove the bread from the oven and preheat the broiler to high. Sprinkle the cheese over the bread and broil for 1 minute. Spoon the tomato mixture over the cheese and broil for 2 minutes longer. Serve warm.

MAKES 16-18 SLICES

RIGHT: Eggplant and Mozzarella Bites, Crostini

TOMATO FOCACCIA

2 *ounces* RECONSTITUTED SUN-DRIED TOMATOES
3 *cups* BREAD FLOUR
1/2 teaspoon SALT
2 *teaspoons* RAPID-RISE ACTIVE-DRY YEAST
6 *tablespoons* OLIVE OIL

Topping
3 *tablespoons* OLIVE OIL
1 *tablespoon* SEA SALT
1 *tablespoon* CHOPPED FRESH BASIL
1 *tablespoon* CHOPPED FRESH THYME

Finely chop the tomatoes. Sift the flour and salt together into a warm bowl, then stir in the yeast. Add the oil, 2/3 cup warm water and tomatoes. Mix together well. Knead on a lightly floured surface for 5 minutes. Roll out into an 11- x 6-inch rectangle. Place on a lightly oiled baking sheet. Make about 20 deep thumb indentations in the dough. Brush with the olive oil, cover with plastic wrap and leave in a warm place for about 40 minutes.

Meanwhile, preheat the oven to 425°F.

Mix together the topping ingredients. Sprinkle over the dough. Bake for about 20 minutes. Best eaten warm.

MAKES 1 LOAF

SUN-DRIED TOMATO LOAF

2 *cups* BREAD FLOUR
1/2 teaspoon SALT
1 1/2 teaspoons RAPID-RISE ACTIVE-DRY YEAST
1/3 cup VERY FINELY CHOPPED SUN-DRIED
TOMATOES IN OIL
2 *tablespoons* OIL FROM THE TOMATO JAR
1 *tablespoon* FINELY CHOPPED FRESH ROSEMARY

Sift the flour and salt into a warm bowl. Stir in the yeast with the remaining ingredients and add 1/2 cup warm water. Mix well. Knead on a lightly floured surface for 5 minutes. Place in a lightly oiled 8- x 4- x 2 1/2-inch bread pan. Cover with plastic wrap and leave in a warm place until double in size.

Meanwhile, preheat the oven to 425°F.

Dust the top of the risen loaf with flour, then bake for about 20 minutes until well risen and golden brown. The bottom should sound hollow when tapped. Leave to cool in the pan for about 10 minutes, then turn out onto a wire rack to cool completely before slicing.

MAKES 1 LOAF

TOP: Tomato Focaccia
BOTTOM: Sun-dried Tomato Loaf

TOMATO AND GARLIC MINI ROLLS

These mini rolls are pictured on page 71 alongside Spiced Roast Beef with Tomato and Ginger Sauce.

1 ounce SUN-DRIED TOMATOES
2 cups WHOLE-WHEAT BREAD FLOUR
1/2 teaspoon SALT
2 tablespoons BUTTER
1 1/2 teaspoons RAPID-RISE ACTIVE-DRY YEAST
1-2 cloves GARLIC, CRUSHED

To Glaze
BEATEN EGG
SESAME SEEDS

Drain the tomatoes well and chop them finely. Sift the flour and salt together into a warm bowl. Cut in the butter and stir in the yeast. Add the garlic and tomato, then add up to 2/3 cup warm water to form a soft, but not sticky, dough. Knead on a lightly floured surface for 5 minutes. Divide the dough into 12 pieces and shape into 4-inch rolls. Make 3 deep scissor snips down the length of each roll. Place on a lightly oiled baking sheet. Cover with oiled plastic wrap and leave in a warm place until double in size.

Meanwhile, preheat the oven to 425°F. Brush the rolls with beaten egg, then sprinkle sesame seeds over the top. Bake for about 12 minutes. Leave to cool on the baking sheet for a few minutes, then turn out onto a wire rack to cool completely. MAKES 12 ROLLS

MEXICAN TACOS

2 tablespoons VEGETABLE OIL
1 ONION, CHOPPED
2 cloves GARLIC, CHOPPED
1 pound TOMATOES, PEELED AND CHOPPED
2 GREEN CHILIES, SEEDED AND SLICED
1/2 teaspoon HOT-PEPPER SAUCE
1 cup DICED COOKED CHICKEN
8 TACO SHELLS
1 cup SHREDDED LETTUCE
1/3 cup GRATED CHEDDAR CHEESE
8 RIPE OLIVES

Heat the oil in a pan and cook the onion and garlic gently for 3 minutes. Add the tomatoes, chilies and hot-pepper sauce. Cover and simmer very gently for 12 minutes until the sauce is reduced to a pulp. Stir in the chicken. Remove from heat. Cover and set aside for 1 hour to let the flavors blend.

Meanwhile, preheat the oven to 350°F. Heat the taco shells for 2-3 minutes. Meanwhile, reheat the tomato mixture. Divide the shredded lettuce between each taco shell. Spoon the tomato mixture over. Sprinkle the grated cheese over and top each taco with an olive.

MAKES 8 TACOS

RIGHT: Mexican Tacos

CHEESE-STUFFED TOMATOES

❉

12 TOMATOES
1¹/3 *cups* GRATED GRUYÈRE CHEESE
1 teaspoon DIJON MUSTARD
1 clove GARLIC, CRUSHED
good pinch CAYENNE PEPPER
1 teaspoon WHITE WINE
³/4 *cup* FRESH WHITE BREAD CRUMBS
1 tablespoon OLIVE OIL
4 slices TOAST, TO SERVE

Preheat the oven to 350°F. Cut the tops off the tomatoes and scoop out the seeds and flesh. Season the tomato insides with salt and pepper, then stand them upside down to drain on paper towels. Heat the cheese very gently in a pan. Remove from heat and stir in the mustard, garlic, cayenne and white wine.

Arrange the tomatoes in a greased roasting pan. Fill each tomato with the cheese mixture, sprinkle the bread crumbs over and drizzle the oil over. Bake for 15-20 minutes. Serve on toast with vegetables or a salad.

SERVES 4

STUFFED BEEFSTEAK TOMATOES

❉

4 LARGE BEEFSTEAK TOMATOES
SALT AND PEPPER
2 slices BACON
1¹/2 *cups* FINELY CHOPPED BROWN MUSHROOMS
4 LARGE EGGS
2 tablespoons BUTTER
4 slices TOAST, TO SERVE

Preheat the oven to 350°F. Cut the tops off the tomatoes and scoop out the seeds and flesh. Season the tomato insides with salt and pepper, then stand upside down to drain on paper towels. Dry-fry the bacon until crisp. Remove from the pan and set aside. Put the mushrooms in the pan and cook quickly until crisp and golden. Remove from heat. Chop the bacon.

Place the tomatoes in a greased baking dish. Divide the bacon and mushrooms between the tomatoes and gently break an egg into each tomato. Dot with butter and bake for 15-18 minutes, until the eggs are set. Serve with toast.

SERVES 4

TOP: Cheese-stuffed Tomatoes
BOTTOM: Stuffed Beefsteak Tomatoes

SUPPER DISHES

Tomatoes complement pizza, pasta, omelets and cheese dishes. Your family and friends will also enjoy Crispy Bacon Phyllo Pie, Deviled Chicken Baked in Foil and Hungarian Goulash, or a variation of macaroni and cheese, spiced up with Worcestershire sauce and a pinch of cayenne pepper.

TOMATO PIZZA

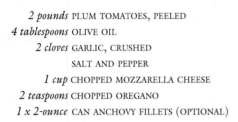

2 pounds PLUM TOMATOES, PEELED
4 tablespoons OLIVE OIL
2 cloves GARLIC, CRUSHED
SALT AND PEPPER
1 cup CHOPPED MOZZARELLA CHEESE
2 teaspoons CHOPPED OREGANO
1 x 2-ounce CAN ANCHOVY FILLETS (OPTIONAL)

Pizza Base
1/2 ounce FRESH YEAST
2 1/4 cups BREAD FLOUR
1 teaspoon SALT
2 tablespoons OLIVE OIL
4 tablespoons MILK

To make the topping, slice half the tomatoes and chop the remainder. Heat half the oil in a pan and fry the garlic for 30 seconds. Add the chopped tomatoes. Cover and simmer for 10 minutes, until reduced to a dry pulp. Season and cool.

To make the pizza base, cream the fresh yeast with 2 tablespoons warm water. Sift the flour and salt into a bowl, make a well in the center and pour in the yeast, oil and half the milk. Mix to a firm dough, adding more milk if necessary. Knead for 5 minutes. Cover and leave to rise in a warm place until double in size.

Meanwhile, preheat the oven to 425°F.

Knead the dough for 2 minutes, then cut it in half and roll each piece into an 8- to 9-inch circle. Place the pizza bases on oiled pizza pans or baking trays. Brush with oil. Cover with the tomato topping. Arrange the fresh tomato slices over each pizza. Sprinkle the mozzarella and oregano over.

If adding the anchovies, drain them and use a sharp knife to slit each fillet in half lengthwise. Arrange the anchovy fillets on the pizzas before the mozzarella. Drizzle the remaining oil over the pizzas and bake for 20-25 minutes. MAKES 2 PIZZAS

RIGHT: Tomato Pizza

CRISPY BACON-PHYLLO PIE

✺

Semolina is the ground endosperm of durum wheat kernels, the type of wheat used to make Italian pasta. You will find it in Italian grocery stores and health-food stores.

6 tablespoons	UNSALTED BUTTER
1 tablespoon	VEGETABLE OIL
2	LARGE ONIONS, THINLY SLICED
1 tablespoon	CUMIN SEEDS
1 x 8-ounce package	PHYLLO PASTRY DOUGH
3 tablespoons	SEMOLINA
1 pound	PLUM TOMATOES, PEELED, QUARTERED AND SEEDED
1 pound	UNSMOKED SLAB BACON SLICES, COOKED UNTIL FAIRLY CRISP AND WELL DRAINED

Preheat the oven to 375°F. Melt 2 tablespoons of the butter with the oil. Add the onions and cook in a covered pan for 15-20 minutes, stirring occasionally, until golden brown. Stir in the cumin seeds and cook for 1 minute longer. Melt the remaining butter in a separate saucepan.

Arrange 9 phyllo pastry sheets in a 9-inch loose-bottomed tart pan, so about one-third of each sheet hangs over the edge. Brush each with a little melted butter. Sprinkle semolina over the bottom, then top with the tomatoes, bacon and cooked onions. Bring the dough up and arrange in loose folds over the filling. Arrange the remaining sheets on top in loose folds to completely cover the filling, brushing with butter while folding the dough. Bake for 25-30 minutes. SERVES 4

TOMATO AND CHEESE PICNIC PIE

✺

12 ounces prepared	PIECRUST DOUGH
2 tablespoons	VEGETABLE OIL
1	SMALL ONION, THINLY SLICED
2 tablespoons	ALL-PURPOSE FLOUR
good pinch	BLACK PEPPER AND MUSTARD POWDER
12 ounces	TOMATOES, PEELED AND SLICED
1½ cups	GRATED CHEDDAR CHEESE
	MILK FOR BRUSHING

Preheat the oven to 400°F. Divide the dough in half. Roll out and use half to line a 9-inch pie plate. Reserve the other half for the lid.

Heat the oil and fry the onion until soft and lightly golden. Meanwhile, mix the flour, pepper and mustard powder together. Stir into the softened onions and add the tomatoes. Mix well. Arrange half the cheese over the dough bottom, cover with the tomato mixture, then the rest of the cheese. Roll out the remaining dough and place on top like a lid. Seal the edges well, brush the top with milk and bake for 30 minutes. Leave to cool on a wire rack. Serve cool. SERVES 4-6

TOP: Crispy Bacon-Phyllo Pie
BOTTOM: Tomato and Cheese Picnic Pie

PIQUANT LAMB

8 *ounces* TOMATOES, PEELED AND CHOPPED
1 LARGE ONION, SLICED INTO THIN WEDGES
3 *tablespoons* LAMB STOCK
3 BAY LEAVES
12 *ounces* LEAN LAMB, CUT INTO STRIPS
5 *cups* HALVED CLOSED-CAP MUSHROOMS
1¹/₃ *cups* CARROTS CUT INTO THICK STICKS
2 *tablespoons* CAPERS, DRAINED
2 *tablespoons* TOMATO PASTE

Place the tomatoes, onion, stock, bay leaves and lamb in a large skillet. Bring to a boil, then cover and simmer for 5 minutes. Add the mushrooms and cook for 10 minutes. Add the carrots and capers and cook for 5 minutes longer. Stir in the tomato paste.

Cook, uncovered, over high heat for 2-3 minutes to reduce some of the liquid. Remove the bay leaves before serving. SERVES 4

GREEK STUFFED TOMATOES

8 BEEFSTEAK TOMATOES
2 *tablespoons* OLIVE OIL
1 ONION, FINELY CHOPPED
1 *clove* GARLIC, CHOPPED
1¹/₄ *cups* ARBORIO RICE
3³/₄ *cups* CHICKEN STOCK, HOT
1¹/₂ *cups* FINELY CHOPPED COOKED LAMB
2 *tablespoons* DRIED CURRANTS OR RAISINS
1 *tablespoon* CHOPPED FRESH THYME

Preheat the oven to 350°F.

Cut the tops off the tomatoes and scoop out the seeds and flesh. Season the tomato insides with salt and pepper, then stand them upside down to drain on paper towels.

Heat half the oil in a pan and cook the onion and garlic for 2 minutes. Add the rice and stir over low heat for 2 minutes. Add 1¹/₄ cups of the stock and cook gently, stirring, until the liquid has been absorbed. Repeat as before with the next 1¹/₄ cups stock and again with the final amount of stock. Stir in the lamb, currants or raisins and thyme.

Arrange the tomatoes in a greased roasting pan. Fill each tomato with the rice mixture. Drizzle the remaining oil over. Bake for 30 minutes. SERVES 4

TOP: *Piquant Lamb*
BOTTOM: *Greek Stuffed Tomatoes*

DEVILED CHICKEN BAKED IN FOIL

4 SUN-DRIED TOMATOES IN OIL, DRAINED
AND CHOPPED

4 tablespoons TOMATO CHUTNEY

1 tablespoon WHOLE-GRAIN MUSTARD

1 cup FRESH WHITE BREAD CRUMBS

4 BONELESS CHICKEN BREAST HALVES, SKINNED

4 teaspoons OIL FROM JAR OF SUN-DRIED TOMATOES

Preheat 375°F. Mix the sun-dried tomatoes, chutney, mustard and bread crumbs together. Make 4 deep slits in each piece of chicken. Spread the deviled mixture over the top. Brush pieces of foil each large enough to completely enclose a piece of chicken with the oil.

Place a chicken breast on each piece of foil. Drizzle any remaining oil over the top. Fold the foil over to make 4 loose packages. Transfer to a baking sheet. Cook in the oven for 25 minutes. Open the foil packages and cook for 5 minutes longer. SERVES 4

CHICKEN CASSEROLE

This dish can either be cooked in the oven at 350°F for 30 minutes, or on top of the stove.

3 tablespoons VEGETABLE OIL

1 LARGE ONION, CHOPPED

4 CHICKEN PORTIONS

1/2 cup ALL-PURPOSE FLOUR

1 x 14-ounce CAN CHOPPED PEELED TOMATOES

1 teaspoon ITALIAN SEASONING

SALT AND PEPPER

Heat the oil in a large flameproof casserole. Fry the onion for 3 minutes. Coat the chicken portions in flour. Add the chicken to the pan and brown on both sides. Pour the tomatoes over. Fill the empty tomato can with water and pour it into the pan. Stir in the herbs. Season.

Cover the casserole and simmer for 30 minutes, adding a little extra boiling water if it simmers too rapidly, or transfer to a preheated oven. SERVES 4

RIGHT: Deviled Chicken Baked in Foil

STUFFED CRÊPES

8 CRÊPES, PRECOOKED
2 tablespoons MARGARINE
1/2 cup ALL-PURPOSE FLOUR
1/4 cup plus 2 tablespoons MILK
2 cups DICED COOKED CHICKEN
8 ounces TOMATOES, PEELED AND SLICED
1/2 cup GRATED CHEDDAR CHEESE

Preheat the oven to 400°F.

Warm the crêpes in the oven. Melt the margarine in a saucepan, then stir in the flour and cook for 2 minutes. Add the milk slowly, stirring constantly. Bring to a boil, then remove from the heat and leave to cool. Stir in the chicken.

Divide the mixture between the crêpes and roll up. Place in a greased baking dish. Top with the tomatoes and cheese and bake for 30 minutes.   SERVES 4

EGGS FLAMENCO

2 tablespoons OLIVE OIL
1 LARGE ONION, SLICED
2 cloves GARLIC, CHOPPED
8 ounces TOMATOES, PEELED AND SLICED
1 1/2 cups SLICED CLOSED-CAP MUSHROOMS
1/2 teaspoon HOT-PEPPER SAUCE
1/2 cup COOKED PEAS
3 ounces GARLIC SAUSAGE, SLICED AND EACH
    SLICE QUARTERED
1 cup DICED COOKED HAM
4 large EGGS
1 small RED BELL PEPPER, CHOPPED

Preheat the oven to 400°F. Heat the oil in a saucepan and fry the onion and garlic until tender but not brown. Add the tomatoes, mushrooms and hot-pepper sauce and cook for 5 minutes. Add the peas, garlic sausage and ham and heat thoroughly, stirring constantly.

Turn into a shallow 9-inch baking dish and smooth the mixture to make it level. Make 4 slight indents with the back of a wooden spoon. Break the eggs over the top of the vegetable mixture and sprinkle with chopped red pepper. Bake for 10-15 minutes or until the whites of the eggs are set.   SERVES 4

RIGHT: Eggs Flamenco

PESTO SAUCE

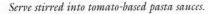

Serve stirred into tomato-based pasta sauces.

3/4 cup CHOPPED BASIL

2 cloves GARLIC, CRUSHED

1/3 cup PINE NUTS, VERY FINELY CHOPPED

1 BEEFSTEAK TOMATO, PEELED, SEEDED AND FINELY CHOPPED

1/2 cup GRATED PARMESAN CHEESE

2/3 cup OLIVE OIL

Place the basil in a mortar and crush with the pestle. Add the garlic and pine nuts and pound again. Gradually add the tomato and cheese, pounding constantly until smooth. Transfer to a bowl and slowly beat in the olive oil, drop-by-drop, until the mixture becomes a smooth sauce. Store in an airtight container in the refrigerator.   MAKES ABOUT 2 CUPS

PASTA SAUCE

Two sliced chilies or 1 teaspoon hot-pepper sauce can be added to the tomatoes. Alternatively, add 1 tablespoon drained capers or 6 ripe olives chopped with the oregano.

3 tablespoons OLIVE OIL

1 RED ONION, FINELY CHOPPED

1 clove GARLIC, FINELY CHOPPED

2 pounds PLUM TOMATOES, PEELED AND CHOPPED

2 stems FRESH OREGANO

1/2 teaspoon SALT

1/4 teaspoon SUGAR

1/4 teaspoon BLACK PEPPER

1 teaspoon RED-WINE VINEGAR

Heat the oil in a large pan. Fry the onion and garlic for 5 minutes. Add the tomatoes. Slowly bring to a boil, then cover and simmer for 8 minutes.

Strip the leaves from the oregano stems and chop the leaves. Add to the tomato sauce with salt, sugar, pepper and vinegar. Simmer for 2 minutes longer. Serve with cooked pasta.   SERVES 4

TOP: Pesto Sauce
BOTTOM: Pasta Sauce

SPICY MACARONI AND CHEESE

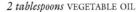

2 tablespoons VEGETABLE OIL
1 LARGE ONION, FINELY CHOPPED
1 GREEN BELL PEPPER, SEEDED AND CHOPPED
1 cup CHOPPED SLAB BACON,
1½ cups SLICED CLOSED-CAP MUSHROOMS
1 x 14-ounce CAN CRUSHED TOMATOES
4 tablespoons TOMATO PASTE
2 tablespoons WORCESTERSHIRE SAUCE
½ teaspoon CAYENNE PEPPER
1 x 7-ounce CAN WHOLE-KERNEL CORN, DRAINED
2 cups MACARONI, COOKED AND DRAINED
1 cup GRATED SHARP CHEDDAR CHEESE
¼ cup DRIED BREAD CRUMBS

Heat the oil and cook the onion and pepper until just soft. Add the bacon and cook for 2 minutes. Add the mushrooms and cook for one minute longer. Stir in the tomatoes, tomato paste, Worcestershire sauce, cayenne, corn and cooked macaroni, then cook over low heat for 5 minutes. Stir in three-quarters of the cheese. Spoon into a warmed flameproof dish.

Preheat the broiler. Mix the remaining cheese and bread crumbs together, then sprinkle them over the top of the macaroni mixture. Broil until the cheese melts and turns golden brown. SERVES 4

FISH PIE

4 large EGGS
1½ pounds POTATOES
12 ounces COD OR HADDOCK FILLET, SKINNED AND DICED
12 ounces SMOKED COD OR HADDOCK FILLET, SKINNED AND DICED
1 LEEK, THINLY SLICED
1 cup FROZEN PEAS, THAWED
⅔ cup PURÉED AND STRAINED TOMATOES
1 pound TOMATOES, PEELED AND SLICED
SALT AND PEPPER
2 tablespoons CHOPPED FRESH PARSLEY
¾ cup GRATED CHEDDAR CHEESE
1 tablespoon MILK (OPTIONAL)

Preheat the oven to 375°F. Hard-cook the eggs for 10 minutes. Boil the potatoes until tender.

Meanwhile, put the fish in a greased 2¼-quart casserole. Add the leek and peas and pour the tomatoes over. Arrange a layer of sliced tomatoes on top. Shell the eggs, cut them into quarters and place on top of the tomatoes, yolks uppermost. Season and sprinkle the parsley over.

Mash the potatoes and beat in half the cheese and a little milk if necessary to make a creamy consistency. Use a decorating bag with a large tip to pipe the potato in a lattice pattern on top of the pie. Sprinkle the remaining grated cheese over. Bake for 45-55 minutes.

SERVES 6

TOP: *Spicy Macaroni and Cheese*
BOTTOM: *Fish Pie*

ROGAN JOSH

This curry is best made the day before and reheated before serving.

2 LARGE ONIONS, CHOPPED

3 tablespoons VEGETABLE OIL

3 cloves GARLIC, CHOPPED

2-4 GREEN CHILIES, SEEDED AND SLICED

1 bunch SCALLIONS, FINELY SLICED

2 pounds STEWING LAMB, CUT INTO 1-INCH CUBES

4 teaspoons GROUND CUMIN

2 teaspoons GROUND CORIANDER

1 teaspoon TURMERIC

1 teaspoon CAYENNE PEPPER

2 pounds TOMATOES, PEELED AND CHOPPED

1½ cups FINELY SHREDDED SPINACH

To serve

2 tablespoons OIL

1 pound TOMATOES, QUARTERED

1 teaspoon GROUND CUMIN

1¾ cups BASMATI OR OTHER LONG-GRAIN RICE, COOKED

Put the onions in a pan with 2½ cups water. Bring to a boil, then simmer for 1 hour until the onions are tender and the liquid has evaporated.

Preheat the oven to 325°F. Meanwhile, heat the oil in another pan and cook the garlic, chilies and scallions for 5 minutes. Add the lamb and spices and brown the lamb thoroughly. Transfer to a casserole. Add the tomatoes and cooked onions. Stir well and season. Cover and cook in the oven for 1¾ hours.

Stir in the spinach and return to the oven. Cook for 15 minutes longer or until the meat is tender.

To serve, heat the oil in a skillet. Add the tomatoes and sprinkle the cumin over. Stir-fry for 15 minutes. Serve the tomatoes lightly mixed into the reheated curry. Serve with rice.   SERVES 6

RIGHT: Rogan Josh

HUNGARIAN GOULASH

3 tablespoons VEGETABLE OIL
2 LARGE ONIONS, SLICED
2 cloves GARLIC, SLICED
2 teaspoons ALL-PURPOSE FLOUR
1½ tablespoons PAPRIKA
2 pounds BONELESS PORK SHOULDER, CUBED
1 cup RED WINE
1 x 14-ounce CAN CHOPPED, PEELED TOMATOES
1 LARGE GREEN BELL PEPPER, SEEDED AND SLICED
1 teaspoon DRIED THYME
2 BAY LEAVES
SALT AND PEPPER
3 cups SLICED CLOSED-CAP MUSHROOMS

Preheat the oven to 325°F. Heat 2 tablespoons of the oil in a large pan and gently fry the onions and garlic for 5 minutes. Meanwhile, mix the flour and paprika together and coat the pork with this mixture. Transfer the onions and garlic to a casserole. Add the remaining oil to the pan, then cook the pork briskly for 5 minutes to brown well. Transfer to the casserole. Add the wine, tomatoes, green bell pepper and herbs. Season, cover and cook in the oven for 1½ hours.

Add the mushrooms and cook for 15 minutes longer or until the pork is tender.   SERVES 6

STIFADO

6 tablespoons VEGETABLE OIL
2 pounds ONIONS, CHOPPED
4 cloves GARLIC, CHOPPED
2 pounds STEWING BEEF, CUT INTO 1-INCH CUBES
2 pounds PLUM TOMATOES, PEELED AND CHOPPED
3 tablespoons TOMATO PASTE
1 cup RED WINE
SALT AND PEPPER

Preheat the oven to 300°F. Heat 4 tablespoons of the oil in a large pan. Gently cook the onions and garlic for 15 minutes until tender and reduced by half. Transfer to a large casserole.

Heat the remaining oil in pan and brown the beef. Transfer to the casserole and add the tomatoes and tomato paste and stir together well. Pour the wine over, and season. Cover with a tight-fitting lid and cook in the oven for 5 hours until the meat is tender and the sauce reduced to resemble the consistency of jam.

SERVES 6-8

TOP: Hungarian Goulash
BOTTOM: Stifado

Texan Chicken

If using a turkey, instead of a chicken, double the quantity of the other ingredients.

1x 3-pound	CHICKEN
1 teaspoon	OIL
1 teaspoon	PAPRIKA
1 pound	TOMATOES, HALVED
	Sauce
2 tablespoons	TOMATO PASTE
1 tablespoon	RED-WINE VINEGAR
1 teaspoon	SUGAR
½ teaspoon	WORCESTERSHIRE SAUCE
¼ teaspoon	HOT-PEPPER SAUCE
1 teaspoon	PAPRIKA
½ teaspoon	CHILI POWDER
¼ teaspoon	GROUND BLACK PEPPER
¼ teaspoon	SALT
1 clove	GARLIC, CRUSHED

Gently ease the skin away from the chicken breast, being careful not to tear the skin. Mix the sauce ingredients together and spoon the mixture under the skin, easing it along the whole breast. Refrigerate for 6 hours to let the sauce flavor the chicken.

Preheat the oven to 375°F. Rub the chicken all over with oil and paprika. Transfer to a roasting pan and roast for 1 hour.

Remove from the oven and drain off excess fat from the roasting pan. Arrange the tomatoes, cut sides up, around the chicken. Baste the tomatoes with juices in the roasting pan. Return to oven and cook for 20 minutes longer. Lift the chicken and tomatoes out of the roasting pan. Use the juices in the roasting pan to make the gravy.

SERVES 4

Fish Creole

juice of 2	LIMES
1½ pounds	COD FILLET, SKINNED AND CUT INTO CHUNKS
2 cloves	GARLIC
8	SCALLIONS, CHOPPED
2 tablespoons	VEGETABLE OIL
2	GREEN CHILIES, SEEDED AND THINLY SLICED
1½ pounds	TOMATOES, PEELED AND SLICED
6	SUN-DRIED TOMATOES IN OIL, DRAINED AND CHOPPED
⅔ cup	WHITE WINE
¼-½ teaspoon	HOT-PEPPER SAUCE
½ cup	ALL-PURPOSE FLOUR
	GREEN SALAD, TO SERVE

Preheat the oven to 400°F. Pour the lime juice over the fish. Marinate for 20 minutes.

Meanwhile, fry the garlic and scallions in half the oil. Add the chilies, and fresh and dried tomatoes and simmer for 10 minutes. Add the wine and simmer for 5 minutes longer. Transfer to a shallow baking dish. Season with the hot-pepper sauce and set aside.

Strain the marinade and pat the fish dry on paper towels. Coat the fish in flour and fry gently in the remaining oil until golden brown but not cooked through. Lay the fish on top of the tomatoes. Cover and cook for 10 minutes.

SERVES 4

RIGHT: Fish Creole

ENTERTAINING

Greet guests with a cocktail and pass around tomatoes stuffed with quails eggs. For a main course, try Veal Parmigiana, Spiced Sirloin Steak or Tomato Soufflé. Many tomato dishes can be prepared in advance, avoiding a last-minute panic before friends or family arrive.

BLOODY MARY

2	ICE CUBES
2 measures	VODKA
1/2 cup	TOMATO JUICE
few drops	LEMON JUICE
	CELERY SALT
few drops	HOT-PEPPER SAUCE
few drops	WORCESTERSHIRE SAUCE
few drops	SHERRY
	FRESHLY GROUND PEPPER

Place all the ingredients in a pitcher and mix well with a fork. Pour into a glass.   SERVES 1

CHEESE AND TOMATO D'ARTOIS

1 pound	FROZEN PUFF PASTRY DOUGH, DEFROSTED
	Filling
2 tablespoons	BUTTER, SOFTENED
1 pound	TOMATOES, PEELED, SEEDED AND FINELY CHOPPED
1 x 2-ounce	CAN ANCHOVY FILLETS, DRAINED AND CHOPPED
2 cups	GRATED CHEDDAR CHEESE
1 large	EGG
pinch	CAYENNE PEPPER
little	MILK, TO GLAZE
	SESAME SEEDS

Preheat the oven to 425°F. Roll out the dough into a 12- x 16-inch rectangle. Cut lengthwise to make 4 pieces of dough, each 12- x 4-inches. Place 2 pieces on a large baking sheet that has been wetted with water.

To make the filling, cream the butter, then add the tomatoes, anchovies, cheese, egg and cayenne to taste. Mix together well, then spread over the dough on the baking sheet. Damp the edges and cover with remaining dough. Seal the edges well. Glaze the tops with a little milk and sprinkle with sesame seeds. Bake for about 25 minutes or until golden, changing shelf positions about half way through the cooking. Cool until cold. Cut into 1-inch fingers. Serve warm.   MAKES 24

Top: Bloody Mary

Bottom: Cheese and Tomato d'Artois

STILTON-STUFFED CHERRY TOMATOES

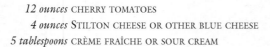

12 ounces CHERRY TOMATOES
4 ounces STILTON CHEESE OR OTHER BLUE CHEESE
5 tablespoons CRÈME FRAÎCHE OR SOUR CREAM

Slice the tops off the tomatoes. Use a sharp knife to remove the core and seeds. Place the tomatoes upside down on paper towels to drain.

Break the Stilton down with a fork into small crumbs, then blend in the crème fraîche or sour cream. Cut a very small slice off the base of each tomato. Use a decorating bag with a star tip, to pipe the Stilton mixture into each tomato.   MAKES ABOUT 30

QUAILS' EGGS IN TOMATO NESTS

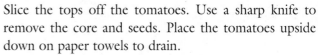

12 QUAILS' EGGS
24 CHERRY TOMATOES
1 teaspoon CAYENNE PEPPER

Place the eggs in a pan of cold water and slowly bring to a boil. Simmer for 3 minutes. Plunge into cold water.

Halve the tomatoes and remove cores and seeds. Place the tomatoes upside down on paper towels to drain.

Shell the eggs and cut each egg in half. Cut a very small slice off the bottom of each half tomato. Fill each half tomato with halved eggs. Sprinkle with cayenne.

MAKES 24

TOP: Stilton-stuffed Tomatoes
BOTTOM: Quails' Eggs in Tomato Nests

POACHED QUAIL WITH MADEIRA WINE SAUCE

8 x 4-ounce QUAILS, TRUSSED
1/4 cup ALL-PURPOSE FLOUR
2 tablespoons BUTTER
1 tablespoon OLIVE OIL
8 rounds WHITE BREAD
2 tablespoons MADEIRA WINE

Sauce
1 pound TOMATOES, PEELED, SEEDED AND CHOPPED
1 clove GARLIC, CRUSHED
2 tablespoons OLIVE OIL
sprig FRESH PARSLEY
SALT AND PEPPER

Stock
1 1/4 cups FRESH CHICKEN STOCK
1 ONION, CHOPPED
1 CARROT, CHOPPED
1 BAY LEAF

To make the sauce, put the tomatoes in a saucepan with the garlic, oil and parsley. Season, cover and simmer for 30 minutes.

Remove the parsley sprig from the tomatoes and strain the tomato sauce through a nylon strainer into a bowl. Keep warm.

Meanwhile, pour the chicken stock into another saucepan, add the onion, carrot and bay leaf. Bring to a boil, then simmer for 20 minutes.

Dust the quails with the flour. Melt the butter with the oil in a skillet, then gently brown the quails, turning regularly, for 10 minutes. Drain off any excess fat. Turn the quails on their sides. Strain the stock into the skillet. Cover and cook very slowly for 10 minutes. Turn the quails to cook on the other side for 5 minutes longer. Pierce with a sharp knife; the juices should be clear.

Meanwhile, toast the bread. Remove trussing strings from the quails. Place the toast on a warm serving dish and top with the cooked quails. Reduce the stock in a skillet by boiling fast, uncovered, until there is about 6 tablespoons. Add the prepared tomato sauce. Stir in the Madeira wine. Strain the sauce and serve.   SERVES 4

RIGHT: Poached Quail with Madeira Wine Sauce

SPICED ROAST BEEF WITH TOMATO AND GINGER SAUCE

2 pounds FILET OF BEEF
1 tablespoon MIXED (GREEN, RED, BLACK, WHITE)
PEPPERCORNS, CRUSHED
1¼ cups PLAIN FROMAGE FRAIS

Marinade
2 tablespoons TOMATO PASTE
1 tablespoon RED-WINE VINEGAR
4 tablespoons VEGETABLE OIL
1 tablespoon BROWN SUGAR
1 clove GARLIC, CRUSHED
1½ teaspoons GRATED FRESH GINGERROOT
½ teaspoon SALT

To serve
LOLLO BIONDO LETTUCE
CORN SALAD LEAVES
CHERRY TOMATOES

Mix all the ingredients for the marinade together. Spread over the beef. Sprinkle the crushed peppercorns over the top and lightly press into the beef. Cover and leave to marinate overnight.

Preheat the oven to 475°F. Transfer the beef and juices to a small roasting pan. Roast for 20 minutes, basting occasionally. Reduce the oven temperature to 425°F, then roast for 20 minutes longer for medium beef or 25 minutes for well done. Remove from the roasting pan and leave to cool completely. Strain and reserve juices.

When cool, make a sauce by stirring the juices into the fromage frais. Check the seasoning. With a very sharp knife, cut the beef into very thin slices. Arrange on a platter with the salad leaves and tomatoes. Serve with the sauce. SERVES 6

CHICKEN WITH TOMATO MAYONNAISE

8 CHICKEN PORTIONS, COOKED AND
SKINNED
4 SCALLIONS, FINELY SLICED
SLICED TOMATOES, TO SERVE

Tomato Mayonnaise
3 large EGG YOLKS
1½ teaspoons SUGAR
1 teaspoon ANCHOVY PASTE
1 teaspoon DRY MUSTARD
¼ teaspoon BLACK PEPPER
3 tablespoons TARRAGON VINEGAR
1 cup EXTRA-VIRGIN OLIVE OIL
½ cup PURÉED AND STRAINED TOMATOES

Place all the mayonnaise ingredients, except the oil and strained tomatoes, in a blender or food processor. Blend, then add the oil, a few drops at a time, and blend well. Continue to add oil through the feed tube in a steady stream, blending well until the mayonnaise is a thick spooning consistency. Stir in the strained tomatoes.

Arrange the chicken portions on a serving platter and spoon the tomato mayonnaise over. Sprinkle the scallions over. Serve with sliced tomatoes. SERVES 8

BOTTOM: *Spiced Roast Beef with Tomato and Ginger Sauce*

ROSEMARY-BAKED MACKEREL

1 SMALL ONION, THINLY SLICED

1 APPLE, CORED AND THINLY
   SLICED

8 ounces TOMATOES, PEELED AND CHOPPED

1¼ cups FISH OR CHICKEN STOCK

small sprig FRESH ROSEMARY

dash WORCESTERSHIRE SAUCE

SALT AND PEPPER

4 x 6- to 8-ounce MACKEREL FILLETS

Preheat the oven to 375°F. Place the onion, apple, tomatoes and stock in a saucepan. Add the rosemary and Worcestershire sauce and season. Bring to a boil, then cover and simmer for 10 minutes.

Fold the mackerel fillets in half with the skin side outermost and place in a baking dish. Pour the sauce over the fish. Cover with foil and bake for 20-25 minutes.

SERVES 4

LEMON SOLE EN PAPILLOTE

This recipe also works well with flounder fillets.

8 x 4-ounce LEMON SOLE FILLETS

sprigs FRESH DILL, TO GARNISH

Stuffing

6 ounces CHERRY TOMATOES, SLICED

1 ONION, FINELY CHOPPED

1½ cups FRESH WHITE BREAD CRUMBS

juice of 1 LEMON

1 large EGG YOLK

4 sprigs FRESH DILL, CHOPPED

Preheat the oven to 375°F. Skin the fish fillets. Mix all the stuffing ingredients together. Place a spoonful on each fish fillet and roll up, securing the end of the fillet underneath with a wooden toothpick.

Cut 4 pieces of parchment paper 15 inches square. Place 2 fish fillets on one side of one piece of paper. Fold the other side of the paper over, covering the fish. Fold the edges of the paper together to make a package. Repeat with remaining packages. Place on a baking sheet and cook in the oven for 15 minutes. Open the packages, transfer the fish to serving plates, garnish and serve immediately.

SERVES 4

RIGHT: Rosemary-baked Mackerel

VEAL PARMIGIANA

🍅

Double the quantities for a dinner party main course.

4 x 3-ounce VEAL CUTLETS
1 EGG, BEATEN
1½ cups FRESH WHITE BREAD CRUMBS
½ cup GRATED PARMESAN CHEESE
4 tablespoons OLIVE OIL
1 ONION, CHOPPED
1 clove GARLIC, CHOPPED
1½ pounds TOMATOES, PEELED AND CHOPPED
1 tablespoon TOMATO PASTE
1 teaspoon FRESH THYME LEAVES
4 BASIL LEAVES, CHOPPED
4 tablespoons BUTTER
5 ounces MOZZARELLA CHEESE, SLICED
sprigs BASIL, TO GARNISH

Preheat the oven to 350°F. Dip the veal cutlets in the beaten egg. Mix the bread crumbs with half the Parmesan cheese and use to coat the veal, then set aside.

Heat half the oil in a skillet and fry the onion and garlic for 3 minutes. Add the tomatoes, tomato paste, thyme and basil. Season. Slowly bring to a boil, then cover and simmer for 10 minutes. Transfer the tomato mixture to a shallow baking dish.

Heat the remaining oil and the butter in a skillet and fry the cutlets quickly until golden brown on both sides. Arrange the cutlets and mozzarella in alternate overlapping slices on top of the tomato mixture. Sprinkle the remaining Parmesan over. Bake, uncovered, for 15 minutes. Garnish with basil. SERVES 4

SPICED SIRLOIN STEAK

🍅

1 teaspoon VEGETABLE OIL
4 x 5-ounce SIRLOIN STEAKS
2 LARGE BEEFSTEAK TOMATOES, SLICED
8 ounces OPEN-CAP MUSHROOMS
2 GREEN CHILIES, SEEDED AND SLICED
2 teaspoons FRESH THYME LEAVES
4 BAY LEAVES
1 cup RED WINE
2 teaspoons CORNSTARCH

Preheat the oven to 350°F. Heat the oil in a skillet and quickly brown the steaks on both sides. Transfer to a large, shallow casserole. Top with the sliced tomatoes and mushrooms, cap sides uppermost. Sprinkle the chilies, thyme and bay leaves over. Pour the wine over. Cover and cook in the oven for 30 minutes.

Gently lift the steaks, tomatoes and mushrooms from the casserole. Transfer to a serving dish. Boil the wine mixture to reduce it by about one-third. Mix the cornstarch with a little cold water and stir the mixture into the wine. Return to a boil. Strain and pour over the steaks. Serve with a green salad. SERVES 4

RIGHT: Veal Parmigiana

TOMATO AND CHEESE ROULADE

1 tablespoon BUTTER
1 pound TOMATOES, PEELED AND FINELY CHOPPED
1/4 cup WHOLE-WHEAT FLOUR
3 large EGGS, SEPARATED
1 large EGG WHITE

RADICCHIO AND FRESH TARRAGON, TO SERVE

Filling
1/2 cup GRATED CHEDDAR CHEESE
2 tablespoons TOMATO CHUTNEY
1/2 teaspoon MUSTARD
2 tablespoons CHOPPED WATERCRESS
SALT AND PEPPER

Preheat the oven to 375°F. Lightly grease a 12- x 8-inch jelly-roll pan and line it with baking parchment.

Melt the butter in a pan, then add the tomatoes and cook for about 4 minutes until pulpy. Stir in the flour and cook over low heat for 1 minute. Remove the pan from the heat. Season. Beat in the egg yolks. Beat the egg whites until stiff, but not dry, then fold lightly, but thoroughly, into the tomato mixture. Spread evenly into the prepared pan, making sure that the mixture reaches right to the edges. Bake for about 20 minutes until just set and firm to the touch.

Meanwhile, make the filling. Mix three-quarters of the grated cheese with the chutney, mustard and half the watercress. Season. Quickly invert the baked roulade onto a clean sheet of baking parchment; remove the lining paper. Spread the filling evenly over the roulade and roll up like a jelly roll. Place on an ovenproof serving dish and sprinkle with the remaining watercress and cheese. Return to the oven for 2-3 minutes. Serve sliced, with radicchio and tarragon.   SERVES 4

TOMATO SOUFFLÉ

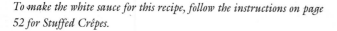

To make the white sauce for this recipe, follow the instructions on page 52 for Stuffed Crêpes.

2 tablespoons MARGARINE
1/4 cup ALL-PURPOSE FLOUR
2/3 cup MILK
2 1/4 cups PURÉED AND STRAINED TOMATOES
4 large EGGS, SEPARATED
1 large EGG WHITE
3 TOMATOES, PEELED, SEEDED AND FINELY CHOPPED

Preheat the oven to 400°F. Make a thick white sauce using the margarine, flour and milk. Remove from the heat and stir in the strained tomatoes and egg yolks. Beat all the egg whites until stiff. Stir the chopped tomatoes into the strained tomato mixture, then gently fold in the beaten egg whites. Pour into a greased 2 1/2-quart soufflé dish. Cook in the oven for 40 minutes. Serve immediately.   SERVES 5

RIGHT: Tomato and Cheese Roulade

VEGETARIAN DISHES

Many cooks now regularly cater for one or more vegetarians, and meatless meals are increasing in popularity. Tomatoes contribute to countless vegetable-based dishes, which can be enjoyed by vegetarians and meat-eaters alike.

VEGETABLE MOUSSAKA

1 LARGE EGGPLANT
SALT AND PEPPER
6 tablespoons VEGETABLE OIL
3 LARGE POTATOES, PEELED AND SLICED
1 LARGE ONION, SLICED
2 pounds TOMATOES, PEELED AND SLICED
3 cups SLICED CLOSED-CAP MUSHROOMS
2 LARGE ZUCCHINI, THINLY SLICED
1 RED BELL PEPPER, SEEDED AND THINLY
SLICED
2 tablespoons MARGARINE
1/4 cup ALL-PURPOSE FLOUR
1 1/4 cups MILK
1 large EGG YOLK
1/2 cup COARSELY GRATED PARMESAN CHEESE

Slice the eggplant and sprinkle the slices with salt. Leave for 30 minutes, then drain. Preheat the oven to 350°F.

Meanwhile, heat 3 tablespoons oil in a large skillet and gently fry the potatoes on both sides for 5 minutes until golden brown. Transfer to a plate and keep warm. Pour the remaining oil into the pan and fry the onion until tender. Add the rinsed and drained eggplant slices and fry for 5 minutes. Add the tomatoes and cook for 5 minutes longer.

Lightly grease a 2 1/2-quart casserole dish. Line the dish with half the potatoes. Add half the tomato and eggplant mixture, followed by a layer of mushrooms, zucchini and red bell pepper, seasoning each layer. Add the remaining tomato and eggplant mixture and top with the remaining potatoes.

Make a white sauce by melting the margarine in a small pan. Stir in the flour and cook for 1 minute. Remove from the heat and gradually stir in the milk. Return to the heat and bring to a boil, stirring constantly. Cool slightly, then stir in the egg yolk. Spread the white sauce over the potatoes and sprinkle on the cheese. Cover and cook in the oven for 1 hour. Remove the lid and cook for 30 minutes longer. Serve with salad.

SERVES 6

RIGHT: Vegetable Moussaka

TOMATO RISOTTO

3 tablespoons OLIVE OIL
1 ONION, FINELY CHOPPED
1 clove GARLIC, CHOPPED
1¼ cups ARBORIO RICE
3¾ cups HOT VEGETABLE STOCK
¾ cup TOMATO JUICE
8 ounces TOMATOES, PEELED AND SEEDED
3 SUN-DRIED TOMATOES IN OIL,
   DRAINED AND CHOPPED
6 LARGE BASIL LEAVES, CHOPPED
¾ cup FINELY CHOPPED MOZZARELLA CHEESE

Heat the oil in a large saucepan. Add onion and garlic and fry until soft. Add the rice and stir over a low heat for 2 minutes. Add 1¼ cups of the stock and cook gently, stirring until the liquid has been absorbed, then add another 1¼ cups of stock. Repeat as before.

Meanwhile, add the tomato juice to the remaining stock and reheat to simmering point. Add the stock and tomato juice to the risotto, together with the fresh and sun-dried tomatoes. Cook, stirring, until the liquid has been absorbed and the rice is tender. Remove from the heat and stir in the basil. Stir in the cheese and serve immediately.   SERVES 3

BOSTON BEANS

1⅓ cups DRIED NAVY BEANS, SOAKED
   OVERNIGHT
1 LARGE RED ONION, SLICED
¾ cup TOMATO JUICE
1¼ cups VEGETABLE STOCK
1 tablespoon BLACK TREACLE OR MOLASSES
1 tablespoon WHOLE-GRAIN MUSTARD
2 tablespoons TOMATO PASTE
8 ounces TOMATOES, QUARTERED
8 ounces CLOSED-CAP MUSHROOMS

Drain the navy beans, then transfer to a saucepan with the onion, tomato juice, stock, black treacle or molasses, mustard and tomato paste. Bring to a boil, then cover and cook for 10 minutes. Reduce the heat and simmer for 1 hour 40 minutes.

Stir in the tomatoes and mushrooms, cover and continue cooking for about 45 minutes or until the beans are soft.   SERVES 4

TOP: *Tomato Risotto*
BOTTOM: *Boston Beans*

TOMATO AND ZUCCHINI LAYER

2 tablespoons VEGETABLE OIL

1 tablespoon BUTTER

1 SMALL ONION, CHOPPED

12 ounces TOMATOES, PEELED AND SLICED

1½ pounds ZUCCHINI, CUT INTO ½-INCH THICK SLICES

SALT AND PEPPER

3 tablespoons MARGARINE

3 tablespoons ALL-PURPOSE FLOUR

2 cups MILK

1 cup GRATED CHEDDAR CHEESE

1 tablespoon BREAD CRUMBS

Preheat the oven to 375°F. Heat the oil and butter in a pan and fry the onion until soft but not browned. Add the tomatoes and fry for 5 minutes. Arrange a layer of zucchini in a greased baking dish followed by a layer of tomatoes. Continue with layers, seasoning with salt and pepper between each layer. Cover and bake for 1 hour until tender.

Meanwhile, make a white sauce with the margarine, flour and milk following the method on page 78. Stir in half the cheese. Drain off the liquid from the baked dish and mix it with the cheese sauce until it is of a coating consistency. Pour over the vegetables. Mix the remaining cheese and bread crumbs together and sprinkle over the top. Place under a hot broiler, or return to the oven, until golden brown and bubbling. Serve immediately.

SERVES 4

TOMATO AND ZUCCHINI TART

6 ounces PREPARED PIECRUST DOUGH

1 pound TOMATOES, PEELED AND SLICED

8 ounces ZUCCHINI, SLICED AND BLANCHED

2 large EGGS

⅔ cup LIGHT CREAM

1 tablespoon CHOPPED FRESH PARSLEY

1 teaspoon SNIPPED FRESH CHIVES

1 teaspoon CHOPPED FRESH SAGE

SALT AND PEPPER

sprig PARSLEY, TO GARNISH

Preheat the oven to 425°F. Roll out the dough thinly and line an 8-inch loose-bottomed tart pan with it. Line the pastry shell with waxed paper and baking beans and bake blind for 15-20 minutes. Reduce the oven temperature to 375°F.

Remove the waxed paper and baking beans. Arrange the tomatoes and zucchini in the pastry shell. Beat the eggs, cream, parsley, chives and sage together. Season. Pour into the pastry shell. Bake for 30-40 minutes until the filling is lightly set. Garnish with parsley. Serve warm.

SERVES 4-6

RIGHT: *Tomato and Zucchini Tart*

TOMATO AND LEEK CROUSTADES

This mixture also fills an 8-inch tart. Increase the cooking time to 15 minutes to bake the tart blind and to 12 minutes for the filling.

2 cups	FRESH WHOLE-WHEAT BREAD CRUMBS
3/4 cup	BLANCHED ALMONDS, FINELY GROUND
1/2 cup	MARGARINE

Filling

2 tablespoons	MARGARINE
1 1/4 cups	SLICED LEEKS
1 tablespoon	ALL-PURPOSE FLOUR
1 cup	CRÈME FRAÎCHE OR SOUR CREAM
8 ounces	TOMATOES, PEELED AND SLICED
1/2 cup	GRATED CHEDDAR CHEESE

Preheat the oven to 375°F. Mix the bread crumbs, almonds and margarine together. Use to line five 4-inch loose-bottomed tart pans. Bake for 10 minutes.

Meanwhile, melt the margarine in a pan and cook the leeks for 5 minutes. Stir in the flour and cook for 1 minute. Stir in the crème fraîche or sour cream and bring slowly to a boil to thicken. Spoon into the tart shells. Top with the sliced tomatoes and sprinkle the cheese over. Return to the oven and bake for 10 minutes longer. Serve hot or cold.   MAKES 5

FRESH TOMATO TART

6 ounces	PREPARED WHOLE-WHEAT PIECRUST DOUGH
1 tablespoon	OLIVE OIL
1 1/2 pounds	TOMATOES, PEELED, SEEDED AND CHOPPED
1 large clove	GARLIC, PEELED AND CRUSHED
3 tablespoons	TOMATO PASTE
1/2 teaspoon	GRATED ORANGE PEEL
1 teaspoon	CHOPPED FRESH MINT
1/2 teaspoon	BROWN SUGAR
	SALT AND PEPPER
3 ounces	MOZZARELLA CHEESE, THINLY SLICED
sprig	BASIL, TO GARNISH

Preheat the oven to 375°F. Roll out the pastry thinly and line an 8-inch loose-bottomed tart pan with it. Line with waxed paper and baking beans. Bake blind for 10 minutes.

Meanwhile, prepare the filling. Heat the oil in a large pan. Add the tomatoes and garlic and simmer for 5 minutes. Add the tomato paste, orange peel, mint and sugar. Cook gently for 10-15 minutes until the sauce is thick and richly colored. Season.

Remove the waxed paper and baking beans from the pastry shell. Spread the tomato mixture evenly in the pastry shell. Top with the slices of cheese. Return to the oven for 30 minutes. Serve warm, cut into wedges and garnish with basil.   SERVES 4-6

RIGHT: Tomato and Leek Croustades

RATATOUILLE

☙

3 tablespoons OLIVE OIL
2 ONIONS, SLICED
2 cloves GARLIC, FINELY CHOPPED
1 LARGE EGGPLANT, CHOPPED
1 pound TOMATOES, QUARTERED
3 ZUCCHINI, SLICED
1 GREEN BELL PEPPER, SEEDED AND CHOPPED
2 tablespoons CHOPPED MIXED FRESH HERBS
2 tablespoons TOMATO PASTE

Slice the eggplant and sprinkle slices with salt. Leave for 30 minutes, then rinse and drain.

Heat the oil and fry the onions and garlic for 2 minutes. Add the eggplant and fry for 5 minutes. Add the tomatoes, zucchini, bell pepper and herbs. Cook very gently for 15 minutes, stirring occasionally. Stir in the tomato paste and season.   SERVES 6

BAKED TOMATOES

☙

These tomatoes are filled with Pesto Sauce and baked in a conventional oven or cooked in a microwave.
8 TOMATOES
5 tablespoons PESTO SAUCE (SEE PAGE 54)

Halve the tomatoes. Scoop out the seeds and flesh. Stand upside down on paper towels to drain for 10 minutes. Spoon some pesto into each tomato half.

To microwave, arrange the tomato halves on a plate. Cover with microwave-safe plastic wrap and cook on Full Power for 3 1/2 minutes.

To bake, preheat the oven to 350°F. Bake for 10 minutes. Serve as a vegetable accompaniment.   SERVES 4

RIGHT: Ratatouille

BROILED TOMATOES

1 pound TOMATOES, HALVED
BUTTER
SALT AND PEPPER
FRESH WHITE BREAD CRUMBS (OPTIONAL)
SNIPPED FRESH CHIVES (OPTIONAL)
GRATED PARMESAN CHEESE (OPTIONAL)

For plain grilled tomatoes, brush the tomatoes with 2 tablespoons melted butter and season. Or, mix $3/4$ cup bread crumbs with 2 tablespoons melted butter. Sprinkle over the tomatoes and season.

Alternatively, mix $3/4$ cup bread crumbs with 2 tablespoons melted butter and snipped chives. Sprinkle over the tomatoes and season.

For a cheesy topping, mix $3/4$ cup bread crumbs with 2 tablespoons melted butter and $1/4$ cup Parmesan cheese. Sprinkle over the tomatoes and season.

For any of the above, place the tomatoes, cut sides up, on a broiler pan. Fix the broiler pan on a low rack and broil under medium heat for 3 minutes. Broil slowly to avoid the tops from burning before the tomatoes are heated through. SERVES 4

TOMATOES AND ZUCCHINI

An excellent way to cook tomatoes and zucchini when there is a glut of them.

3 tablespoons OLIVE OIL
1 1/2 pounds ZUCCHINI, SLICED
1 pound TOMATOES, PEELED AND QUARTERED
4 BASIL LEAVES, CHOPPED
SALT AND PEPPER

Heat the oil in a pan. Fry the zucchini briskly for 10 minutes until golden brown. Lower the heat and add the tomatoes. Cover and simmer for 10 minutes.

Stir in the basil and season well. Serve immediately as a vegetable side dish. Alternatively, cool, transfer to freezer bags, label and freeze. SERVES 6

RIGHT: Broiled Tomatoes

MARINADES, CHUTNEYS AND RELISHES

Late summer is the time to make tomato chutneys, pickles and relishes. The recipes here have been created with the *Sandwiches and Snacks* chapter in mind. Tomatoes add color as well as flavor to marinades for barbecued meat, poultry or fish.

PIQUANT TOMATO MARINADE

For a barbecue, this quantity will marinate 8 chicken drumsticks.

4 tablespoons HONEY
2 tablespoons TOMATO PASTE
2 tablespoons MALT VINEGAR
2 tablespoons SOY SAUCE
1 teaspoon GROUND GINGER
3 drops HOT-PEPPER SAUCE

Gently warm the honey in a saucepan or in the microwave on Medium for 30 seconds. Stir in the remaining ingredients. Use to marinate chicken drumsticks for 6 hours prior to grilling on the barbecue.

TOMATO, ORANGE AND LEMON MARINADE

For a barbecue, this quantity will marinate 20 pork spareribs.

4 tablespoons HONEY
3 tablespoons TOMATO PASTE
3 tablespoons SOY SAUCE
1 teaspoon DIJON MUSTARD
1 clove GARLIC, CRUSHED
3 tablespoons ORANGE JUICE
3 tablespoons LEMON JUICE

Gently warm the honey in a saucepan or in the microwave on Medium for 30 seconds. Stir in the remaining ingredients. Use to marinate spareribs for 6 hours prior to cooking on the barbecue.

TOMATO GLAZE

For grilling meat, poultry or fish on a barbecue.

2 tablespoons TOMATO PASTE
1 tablespoon SOY SAUCE
1 tablespoon OIL

Brush the meat, poultry or fish with the tomato glaze every 5 minutes while the food is grilling on the barbecue.

FROM LEFT TO RIGHT: Piquant Tomato Marinade, Tomato, Orange and Lemon Marinade, Tomato Glaze

GREEN TOMATO CHUTNEY

3 cups CHOPPED ONIONS
2 tablespoons PICKLING SPICE
5 pounds GREEN TOMATOES, PEELED AND
QUARTERED
2 teaspoons SALT
2 1/2 cups MALT VINEGAR
1 pound SUGAR

Put the onions and 2/3 cup water in a large saucepan and cook until soft. Drain off the water. Tie the pickling spice in a cheesecloth bag. Tie firmly to the saucepan handle with the bag inside the pan. Add the tomatoes and salt and bring to a boil. Reduce the heat and simmer for 1 hour, stirring occasionally.

When the mixture thickens, add a little of the malt vinegar. Finally add the remaining malt vinegar and the sugar to the saucepan and cook until the mixture is thick, stirring frequently. When the chutney is ready, remove the cheesecloth bag. Pour the chutney into sterilized hot jars and seal. Store for 1 month before using. Best consumed within 6 months. MAKES 3 POUNDS

RIPE TOMATO CHUTNEY

2 1/2 cups MALT VINEGAR
1 tablespoon PICKLING SPICE
6 pounds RIPE TOMATOES, PEELED AND QUARTERED
2 LARGE ONIONS, CHOPPED
2 teaspoons PAPRIKA
1/4 teaspoon CAYENNE PEPPER
1 tablespoon SALT
1 3/4 cups SUGAR

Make a medium-spiced vinegar by boiling the pickling spice in the vinegar for 10 minutes. Cool. The spices may be left in the cooling vinegar if desired, to increase the spiciness.

Put the tomatoes in a large saucepan with the chopped onions. Heat gently, then simmer to a thick pulp, stirring occasionally. Add half the strained spiced vinegar together with the paprika and cayenne. Sprinkle the salt over and bring to a boil. Cook, uncovered, until thickened.

Meanwhile, heat the remaining strained, spiced vinegar with the sugar until dissolved. Add to the tomatoes. Boil and reduce to a thick pulp. Pour into sterilized, hot jars and seal. Store for 1 month before using. Best consumed within 6 months.

MAKES 4 POUNDS

RIGHT: Ripe Tomato Chutney,
Green Tomato Chutney

GREEN TOMATO PICKLE

3 pounds GREEN TOMATOES, QUARTERED

1/2 SMALL CABBAGE, COARSELY SHREDDED

1 CAULIFLOWER, SEPARATED INTO FLOWERETS

2 CUCUMBERS, DICED

3 cups COARSELY CHOPPED ONIONS

1/2 cup SALT

1 teaspoon PEPPERCORNS

1/2 cup DRY MUSTARD

4 1/2 cups MALT VINEGAR

1 heaped cup SUGAR

1 tablespoon TURMERIC

Layer the tomatoes, cabbage, cauliflower, cucumbers and onions in a bowl with layers of salt in between. Cover and leave to stand overnight.

Drain the vegetables. Tie the peppercorns in a cheesecloth bag. Blend the mustard with 1 1/4 cups of the malt vinegar. Put the blended mustard, vinegar, sugar, turmeric and peppercorns into a large pan. Tie the cheesecloth bag firmly to the saucepan handle so it is immersed in the liquid.

Heat gently, stirring, until the sugar is dissolved, then bring to a boil and boil for about 5 minutes. Add the vegetables and heat through without boiling. Remove the cheesecloth bag. Pack the pickle into sterilized, hot jars and seal. Store for 1 month before using. Best consumed within 6 months. MAKES ABOUT 9 POUNDS

QUICK TOMATO RELISH

1 tablespoon OLIVE OIL

1 bunch SCALLIONS, CHOPPED

4 tablespoons ALL-PURPOSE FLOUR

1 x 14-ounce CAN PEELED TOMATOES

2-3 teaspoons WORCESTERSHIRE SAUCE

SALT AND PEPPER

Heat the oil and gently cook the scallions for 5 minutes. Stir in the flour and cook for 1 minute. Drain the tomatoes, reserving the juice. Gradually stir in the juice. Finely chop the tomatoes and put in the pan. Bring to a boil, stirring. Stir in the Worcestershire sauce and season to taste. Cook for 1 minute. Cool, then chill. Serve with cold meats. SERVES 6

TOP: *Green Tomato Pickle*
BOTTOM: *Quick Tomato Relish*

INDEX